A VISIT TO MADINAH

Prophet Muhammad for Little Hearts

by

SANIYASNAIN KHAN

Goodword**kidz**

Helping you build a family of faith

When Muhammad ﷺ was six years old, his mother, Aminah, decided to take him with her to visit his uncles in Madinah, which was known at that time as Yathrib.

YATHRIB
(Now known as Madinah)

MAKKAH

ARABIA

RED SEA

EGYPT

Yathrib was situated in the midst of volcanic hills in the Hijaz region of western Saudi Arabia about 100 miles (160 km) inland from the Red Sea.

ARABIAN GULF

5

In its early days, it was an oasis famed for the dates from its palm groves.

It was a long journey by caravan, but young Muhammad ﷺ enjoyed meeting his cousins, playing with them and learning to swim.

Muhammad ﷺ and Aminah enjoyed the pleasant climate and the company of their relatives for a month.

But, tragically, on the journey back to Makkah, Aminah fell ill and died. (The Prophet Muhammad's father died a few months before his birth.)

Little Muhammad ﷺ returned home with Aminah's maid, Barakah.

The Prophet Muhammad's grandfather, Abd al-Muttalib, adopted him and took care of him.

Abd al-Muttalib loved Muhammad ﷺ dearly, and felt sure that he would one day be a great man.

All the time that Abd al-Muttalib sat near the Kabah speaking words of wisdom, Muhammad ﷺ, remained by his side. When Abd al-Muttalib fell sick two years later, Muhammad ﷺ attended to him faithfully.

When his grandfather died,
Muhammad ﷺ was adopted
by his uncle, Abu Talib.

Muhammad ﷺ became part of Abu Talib's large family right away, and was his uncle's favourite.